Sage
and
Pine

K. Bruce Jordan

NEWMAN SPRINGS PUBLISHING
320 Broad Street
Red Bank, NJ 07701

First originally published by Newman Springs Publishing 2023

ISBN 978-1-68498-868-6 (Paperback)
ISBN 978-1-68498-869-3 (Digital)

Printed in the United States of America

A very special thanks to the long line of masters of eternal knowledge and wisdom, especially Maharishi Mahesh Yogi. Jai Guru Dev.

Contents

Home

is kind of a haven of relaxation.
like a game preserve or a garden.
a grateful space to come in from the day's work.
and settle back in the enveloping easy chair
to rest awhile.
cool down a spell and warm the heart.
with a boiled cup of milk and clarified butter (ghee)
with a plump, furry friend in the lap…

A place is home to let your thoughts roam freely
and hearken back to ultra-pleasant memories
like skippin' rocks across the river,
shootin' hoops,
flippin' frisbees
with my genial son, Aaron…
to remember odd jobs to do when inspiration hits
or let playful artworks surprise you
with their beauty
or to kick back and shoot darts
at circled dates on the calendar…

A collection of poignant moments is home.
in our mobile world of wonder.
at tomorrow's offering.

dropped in the lap of opportunity.
like a lost pet companion
content to lick your hand
in a kind of quiet communion…

Boise

"The city of trees"
placid people
church steeples
green leaves

Warm and sheltered
by grand and fatherly mountains
overseeing busy vistas

Mothered by fountains
of cool
      clear
           rainbow
                waters

Doves *coo coo* to you

Frilly daffodils
red and yellow tulips too!

Elderberry Time in Idaho

Plate-sized fronds hang ripe and full of BB-like berries of the domestic variety (the wild variety is poisonous).

Plump and firm, dark and purple, bittersweet.

Support stems are snipped, and each cluster is dropped into a tub or basket or bucket.

Later, water is rinsed in as spiders and ladybugs heading for higher ground are carefully picked out…

Then the berries are stripped down into a pan or colander and strained.

The juice is then boiled with pectin and allowed to cool. Stir in sugar to taste.

The precipitate makes the tastiest syrup, jelly, or jam. Guaranteed via experience firsthand. Thanks to my wonderful mother, Lucille.

Every Day Is a New Ball Game

An opportune time
to triple into the gap
of gratitude
and do our dads proud…

using each and all of the appreciable talents
remembered from some hundreds of thousands
of slices of the big apple pie of delight
in new experience on beloved satellite earth
just for everyone's benefit of the doubt.

to make a great theatrical homerun of a hit
into the upper deck of agreed upon accomplishment
via transcendental consciousness no less.

to catch every "high-hopper" for an easy out
every time our number comes up
we are given a challenge.

Forgetting less-than-perfect pitches
is easier
coming from a space of blissful integrity
in eternal Being.

stresses dissolved

all is forgotten

hence forgiven

Let's play Ball!

He Who Has Planted Will Preserve

Grampa was the planter, Gramma the preserver. When he was hoeing weeds, shoveling ditches, changing water, milking cows, feeding chickens, hauling hay, motoring into town to pick up the mail, or traveling into Caldwell to "the sale." I went along, a step or two behind, watching for horses, enjoying the ride in silence, very much admiring his steadiness of mind, listening intently as he hummed his song.

The same with Gramma as she offered us candy, gave us large, white cardboard to draw on, hunted up a puzzle or two to baffle us for hours, getting out the cards or dominoes, admiring her crafts as her eyes sparkled, light-hearted laughter and stories of her youth in Colorado; the Coxes of Wray following her out into the yard and garden as she stopped to pull weeds, point out flowers, snapdragons, pansies; wandering along, charmed by the variety of colors and patterns, inhaling aromas—roses, lilacs, lilies; swinging in the swing; peonies, bleeding hearts, dozens of perfumes permeating, exhilarating the mind and soul, marigolds, daisies, begonias, assured that they will read this some time, hence though they have passed on. Crocus, iris, Otto and Ethel Teichert, morning glories…

Smokey the Bear

Smokey the bear,
Smokey the bear,
Prowlin' and a growlin'
And a sniffin' the air.

He can find a fire
Before it fans to flame.
That's why they call him Smokey.
That is how he got his name.

—U.S. Forest Service
as sung by Arthur Jordan

A Swinger of Birches

I have been also.

We had one in the backyard in Middleton. They are kind of difficult to find in Idaho. Really, I am more of a rider of pines, thanks to the "good eye" of my father's mother, Ann.

From the time I was four or five years young, we would stroll through the forest, looking for the best "bronc" of all to ride.

"There's one!" I would excitedly holler, then quickly shinny out on a half-fallen tree, begin a rhythm with the upper body until that sapling was really "bucking" up and down. Those were the times…

We just cannot say we have lived a full life if we have not once galloped an "Appaloosa" pine.

This Breeze

caresses gently, friend…
"Ole Sol" is rising higher
looking forward to today, maybe
peering up out of mountainous covers, certainly,
radiating orange, warming rays of fiery light…

Those clouds are like cotton-candy for the
Angels this morning…

Fish splash!

An ant explores the pores of this arm,
antennae tweedling, it jeeps on over
down, around, and through the maze
of junglelike grass-blades,
bebops across the top of a paperback book.
Ants, the itinerant, literate laureates…

Fish flips!

Since when were goldfish orange?

The breezy rapids must be stirring
their appetites for aquatic athletics.

fish, the original olympians
breasting their colors…

Ah, what a day,
perfect for t-shirts, cutoffs, all-star
tigerpaw, fleetfeet squeakers,
clip-cloppin' along this concrete sidewalk.
hip-hop, sidestep, turnaround,
trottin' on downtown
to the hit tunes
of a June noon…

Spring Is

blue and green and white with black crows slowly winging by a tangled kite in a tree waves as swallows sail along with breezes chasing gnats…

All smiles, sky-girls ride by on bicycles, pass before the warm orb in the southwest…

Speckled starlings screech from an old elm tree. Airplanes soar over absorbed lovers. A truck rumbles, shifts, rumbles up Capitol boulevard as a pretty blonde lass and her Lassie are wading in the ripples of the otherwise glassy river…

Golden youths scattered there, there flip frisbees run barefoot through luxurious, deep, green grasses…

Spring is shirttails out and waving at shoes kicked off and forgotten…

"Black Sheep" Swan

Gliding upon the pond,
So easily through
This neutral morning…

Calm…
Serene…

Is it by some high spirit
That you can be content?
Faithful, you sail along, alone…
With a full head of esteem…

Unmindful…
Natural…

Leaving your regal self open to everyone,
Like ducks on a pond…

Didja Ever Spread-Eagle

in the tender clover?
stretch out and gaze
at clouds floating over?

Those huge accumulations
of white and gray
assembled in an endless array of faces,
figures going who knew where,
around the world, dropping rain
in familiar places, maybe
gathering steam for other continents
and strange locations, occasionally
offering an architecture far and away
above our highly prized man-made creations
that have their beauty too.
in the overall scheme of things,
for arriving at curious amazement,
true apparitions of wonder, clouds,
for we dreamers of freedom, here
as on foreign shores…

Out in the Barnyard

On a farm in Idaho, cows are in the stanchions, chewing hay and oats while the straddled calves butt and suck the nippled buckets, trying to gulp another drop of wholesome milk.

Milking right along, Pappy fills the pail with bubbly foam as yours truly sits half asleep aboard the bench and holding "ole boss" tail out of his eyes as she tries to express her delight and stir the swarms of magnetic flies. And out in the pigpen, the yearling sow roots and grunts, wiggling her curly tail and flapping her ears forth and back as his majesty braces and raises his brilliant red head in letting the living countryside know he heralds the dawn of a fresh, clean morning, crowing up a song for the sleepy sun, breasting and whisking his wahoo wings. But the sow is not too impressed as she yawns and eats and drinks while the cows are not overly impressed as they munch their hay and oats and look around behind to see just what is taking so long.

When Pappy finally finishes stripping the cows of udder discomfort, he reminds me of caution and "Don't forget, I'm goin' in with pails to strain the milk and separate the cream while you can hay the steers and turn the herd out to graze, bring in the calf buckets. Mom's got buckwheat pancakes all ready to eat."

I say, "Okay." Hungry stomach rumbles in agreement. Surely, but sure slowly, carefully, Brownie and Annie and Susie and Blacky maneuver around, easing their way toward the doorway airing fresh-air freedom to let their creative juices flow to whet a thirst for the fiery goldfish in its water trough world, mirroring warm and wondrous summer acres of easy-rollin' green hill pastures...

Warbles, Trills, and Chirps

Penetrate my privacy,
High and free as children in the park.
It's okay, these backyard arias cheer me.
I was just dreaming, reading, writing
The way I usually do on Saturdays and Sundays
And holidays.

Two weeks after April Fool's Day,
I realize I've been too wrapped up
In the future and the past…
It's time to take the outlet pass
On the fast break for a scrumptious brunch
But not before our artful science
Of healing silence,
Transcendental Meditation…™

The spirit of adventure is strong.
I desire lifesavers, inspired writing.
What's your favorite flavor? Author?
Grape, orange, banana, cherry, Dickensen?
And all of the others? Frost, Emerson?

I want to usurp life the way we do soup.
I want butterscotch pudding from above.
From the loving heart,
The full-sail soul…

Sweet Anonymity

Blessed solitude…
Transformational vacuum of time.
Restful effervescence.
Quiet radiance…

Five days a week,
We find ourselves on stage, performing.
It's nice to have the notoriety,
But freedom really seems to sing,
Ring true
With the colorful spice
Of a life of variety…
One could say the life
Of James Whitcomb Riley.

It's truly a godsend
Observing the weekend
In the wings…

It's a Good Day for a Drive

Let's stretch out and float on our minds
  in the heavens everywhere,
    there's plenty of time…

Almost thought "ole Sol" had blown a fuse,
  forgot how to shine.
    heaven knows those porous clouds
      have been workin' overtime.

Just smell those fresh airs,
  sage and pine
    sure smells clear to me.
      let's pack a repast for tonight.
        buy some gas and groceries
          a hundred miles from here.
            it's a good day for a drive.

Tonight, we could tell true tales
  beside a flickerin' fire,
    sleepily lay down, look up
      at all the moons and stars…

Tomorrow, we could experience
  a warm, easy hike,
    savor a tasty picnic,
      clown around, fall in the river.
        Oh, Babe, it's a good day for a drive.

The Jordan

is a common river.
speaking literally and symbolically
whether here in Boise, Fairfield, or Zimbabwe.
flowing through our hearts and minds
hopefully,
faithfully
giving us some subtle support,
just as in bible times
when infant Moses floated by,
dropped anchor,
and waited in the bulrushes
for those delightful sisters
so cheerful and mild.

Surprizing things live inside of us
and occasionally surface,
complete creations waiting, hoping,
praying to hear the happy laughter
of ideal life.

Each of these poems, then, for all times,
approach a child.

Before Dawn

Unexpectant miners go within,
Transcend…
Highly deep into their quiet brightness.
Lighting candles every one
To collectively turn the world around
In world peace
With utmost ease
And routinely mine for "diamonds"
Of knowledge,
"Rubies"
Of truth,
"Silver"
For the spiritual body,
And "gold"
For the wholistic soul.

Enriched, refreshed,
They emerge beaming,
Giving freely of their natural wealth.

Days of April

Remind me of my mind.
Mother Nature, too, it seems,
Becomes confused at times.

Morning mingles crisp and clear,
Warm breezes comb my hair,
Followed silent by secret cirrus
As ominous cirrocumulus pull the shades
And flip the switch from day to night.

Waltzing with them come whistling winds
Uniting against the lordly mountains.
Gusts die down, silence reigns, lightning cracks!
The overhead reservoir thunders, shudders, pours.

Feeling ecstatic, sensing the power, perhaps,
I bound into the house to close the windows
And watch the waters bathe the home
From stem to stern, from aerial to wheels.

Awakening later, I see "ole Sol," the sun,
And the book is still in my lap
From the unintentional nap I took.
Then realize surprise at Mother Nature.
She, too, can change her mind, you know.

Don't Ever Get Stickers

stuck in your socks.
They itch/hurt like crazy
whenever you try to walk.
sooner or later (I swear)
you'll have to stop
and plop down on a rock
and pluck out those irritators
before you can talk
about all the beauty
there is in a hike
up in the foothills
and stupendous mountains high.

You'll be glidin' along
gazin' for miles and miles
and tellin' tall tales
that'd make Paul Bunyan
and his blue ox small
(and want to hide)
but you really don't care
'cause you feel so good,
'cept for those pesky stickers
needlin' your hairs
and make you wish you'd watch

where you fall
and be more careful of canyon walls. Ahh…

You really don't mind swimmin' rapids
up there, down through whitewater and over
The falls. Ahh…
but all the fun's spoiled
when reminded once more
those darned stickers
are makin' you sore
as with a fish in your pocket
(a rainbow)
you crawl ashore and utter once more,
"Don't ever get stickers stuck in your socks—
Ouch—or shorts!"

I'm a "Thank You"

This day is the day I've been waiting and waiting and
    waiting
But this is the day I'm dating, and playing, and chasing.
But this one… Ah, this one I'm seeing and being and
    freeing
'Cause winter lives a little everywhere.

So stop us and help us to selfless, Oh,
Make this day the way of rays, Oh,
But I'm thirsty and dreamy and hoping, though hope and
    dreams and spiritual and physical thirst are waste of
    haste to most, I know they make me to we and us to I
    to fly…

Not bad or sad are they or me.
We see and feel and know, I think, that later or sooner we'll
    free our freeze.
Ah, but today is the day of players and sayers and prayers
    and prayers of thanks…

✦ ─────── ❧ ─────── ✦

It's My Favorite Season

Except for winter, fall, and spring.
The time is right to swim in sunshine,
Bring about a balance of body and mind,
Drink spring water in the chaise lounge,
Gaze off into the treetops,
Sail out on a dream or a boat or both.
Trod barefoot up a warm, powdery mountain road
with fishin' pole over a shoulder to breathtaking
edge, cool, crystalline lakes, space
and bake a freckled tan upon an unpredictable
mattress of air
till that perfect circle of fire ignites
the horizon as a spark starts a sizzler,
roastin' poetry over a cracklin' campfire
while guitar and harmonica puff up hearts,
marshmallows, hotdogs, ouch/horseflies,
mosquitoes and, above all, alpenglow moonlight…

Bowl Me Over

with a ticklish feather,
knock me out with a perfumed flower,
blast off my cap with the number of light-years
between even two bright stars in the universe.
stagger me with the slow curve of a meteor
or the minute size of a single atom of matter.
give me a "kick in the pants" with a heck of a
wild hike in the high country
above the timberline…
How about a break for a siesta
anywhere near these sweet buckbrush blossoms
beside this giggly creek…

Atop an onslaught of awareness,
I'm barely upright
to matter-of-fact infinity
tonight…

There Is a Story

in the pantleg.
Every dog knows this.
Cats also know this.

They know if we had dinner at the deli,
went wadin' in the river,
just dusted in from the desert,
or floated down from the forest,
and so much more,
like how many hours
since our last bath or shower,
how many days
since we changed our socks, oh gosh,
so much more they know.
(they know)

My "Dog" Purrs

Runs to the front door when I arrive.
His tail doesn't wag, just twitches a bit.
He loves to play ball with a toy mouse.
Follows me around the house with the tip of his tongue
     sticking out.

After dinner, he doesn't sit at my feet. He has to be right
     beside me in the recliner.
Instead of barking at the moon, he just meows,
"Hey, how 'bout a treat?"
He thinks he's people, I bet, or at least equal.

He gets away with more than most. I guess, just like a
     puppy, we're wrapped around his furry little paws.
Our "dog" has the sharpest claws in town.
"Ouch!"

The Spoon That Wouldn't Quit

found its way into my grasp and gulp and waistline.

With the precision of a Hawaiian cliff diver,
I perch on a windy bluff of pleasure
and do a perfect "gainer"
into a carton of irresistable
tin roof sundae.
Ahh, cool, smooth, sweet, and creamy…

If I have a high cholesterol,
it'll be that fast-food spoon's fault.
It's one of those deeply curved jobs.
No surface skimmer, this…

It forces me to eat too quick
and trot in the store for more.
It's a conspiracy, I tell you.

Wonder Why?

What makes a coyote howl
When he sees the risin' moon?
What makes him sit up sad
Amid his blackened blues?
And where in the night
Has he hid his pride?
To sit beneath the stars
And sigh?
And does he wonder why?

What makes a mountain goat
Seek a higher bluff
When he knows that he'd be warmer
Farther down below?
And will he know
When he's reached his peak?
And will he be satisfied?
Will he live to see his kids
Comin' up from behind?
And does he wonder why?

What does that hoot owl see
While glidin' through the night?
Why does he light and hoot and wink

Then fly on by?
Well, some may say that I'm a fool,
And that he is wise.
But tonight, it seems so natural
To sit and wonder why…
Yes, tonight, it seems so natural
To sit and wonder why…

I Put People to Sleep

whenever I chance to speak,
people stop and yawn and go on.
it's okay. I don't mind.
soft-spoken, I'm just tryin' to let actions
do most of the talkin'
in a world where everyone's hummin'
their very own song,
and rightly so…

It's enough to live our own life
in a way we believe is best,
carefully carefree, maybe.

I don't care to bomb people out of the water
with high-flown rhetoric.
sure, I have an ego a-go-go going on
somewhere…

Once in a blue moon,
I "uncork" one of my own
"wild ideas"
for sporting fun.
come on along, if you like.
walk softly with me,

just bein' ourselves,
like everybody else…

Someone said that people
are just like sheep.
Me? I'm just tryin' to keep up
with my own distant dreams.
is that so baaaaad?

The Heart of Joy

is found to be the creative center's source
of every single flower.

Luxurious petals envelop the fragile
filament, anther, stamen, stigma, style,
sepal, pedicel, and invisible liquid
to form
the full, mature fruit
sweetened by many passive moments,
absent
from wind-driven dancing
or solitary tears
of mist.

Deep, sound sleep slowly rises to a cricket symphony.

Colorful songbirds sing solos,
Ahh, fresh air, huh?

Someone's hummin' over an open fire.
Hot water's whistlin' somethin' over a steamed-up teapot.

A few happy campers glide out of their tents.

Scents of maple butter churn interest.
Hearts asimmer, eyes bright, wits honed, we pour hot cups
    o' humor.

With stomachs runnin' on empty,
some of us "dive" into a plate of cakes and come out smilin'
    with milk mustaches (after silent prayer of thanks).

Desirin' more and more is natural (we hear).

The Creator created creation for the increase of happiness.

Oh look, a mountain bluebird!

In Drifts a Mist

ephemeral in these esteemed peaks,
   giving us a disarming embrace, I guess
      a kiss so cool and moist upon the lips
         and neck, face, and hands…

So long "ole Sol" don't hurry, brrr.
   just kiddin' warm the leaves of those
      shiverin' aspen as you inspire her to
         cuddle up a little closer, please…

Our heads are literally in the clouds.
   this mind and body swoon in waves of spirit
      similar to that barely visible eagle-like
         hawk up there, diving and rising
            on invisible currents of supportive air…
We are indeed unflappable in our majesty,
   this mystical, magical day…

In the encouraging light,
   the bloom of our red, rose heart
      is inevitable…

Springtime by the Waterfalls

jubilant leaves are shining too,
whitewater roars its frothy approval…

I sit here on a rock on the bank of the river,
Loving, remembering intimate moments…

The waves can't seem to help themselves.
they always come and go, regardless…

Fulfilling what fell and falls before them,
leading the way for all that follow…

Carried along in the stream of eternity
(an avid, rapid happening, perhaps),
togethering turbulent undertows…

Helpless, I welcome them with open heart,
having so much fun in wonderment
and, surprisingly, not feeling all alone…

Poetry Is a High Dive

into a birdbath of the unknown.
It comes to you from out of the proverbial blue,
helping you feel a little tickled
after it's scribbled
on a flimsy piece of tissue.
It hits you while you're busy trying
to burn water
or pruning your heavy-duty plum tree.

It has some similarity to an air raid, all right.
It kind of thickens in your conscious mind
like jell-o in a bowl
from sense, impressions, feelings, and unusual
word sounds. An island of silence
in activity are often causes.

What it is
is music to the soul
when it's good and magical.
Sometimes, you get an appealing title,
first line, phrase, or main idea.
It is most pleasurable when it flows
on several levels simultaneously.

Above all,
it helps humans love life.
live love.
(like I like it).

A Mile High

in his own world, the sky,
the raptor endures nagging harassment
as territorials trail, dart, assail,
flying aerial acrobatics,
protecting their hatchlings.

The raptor is a hunter
who respects the open air,
sort of a servant of Mother Nature,
balancing this cycle of life in the wild
where one absorbs another,
a high glider quite aware of others
who've never perched on peaks
of natural grandeur.

Simple in his habits,
seldom caring for something sometime,
but everything always
just as it is…

No seeker of fortune, fame, or praise,
just another one who knows his place,
only resting on occasion

to incubate generations
of like altitudes of servitude
for the whole procession…

Soul Desire

is no desire or
is the hub of the universe possibly
of which we are of or
am?

But in the universe are mini-verse seen
                              to see for or
mini-peoples felt
                              to feel for or
mini-rhythms heard
                              to hear for or
mini-aromas sensed
                              to smell better for or
(sunflower seed shells stuck in de teeth)
all speeding onward from the wordless
world of serenity or

spedding from
                    unto the
                              Everything I crave or
force field friends
     to intuit
          to.

Life Is

such a delicate thing.
The softest breath is all that keeps us here
on this plane, this sphere called earth.

The natural life
is as fluid as the air or music or water
or a child's movements full of hopeful promise,
a herald of expression of future-present.
It exhibits tenderness that tantalizes writers
and artists and resourceful scientists.

When noisy day is easily lived
or suddenly done (surprisingly fast),
leaving we philosopher few strewing words
in wonder, praise, and admiration in a poem
or a song or an artful work,
it zeroes home how fascinating life is
with all of its differences and likes
that it should finally, after a galaxy of lives,
happiness brings strong and continuous,
bright as a rainbow, home to radiant
appreciation
as fruit from blossoms
blooms from spring shine,
life is truly a delicate being.

The Fidget Rock

Well off is the one
   who has happened upon a fidget rock
      while balancing on a boulder.

We don't have to be beside a rippled river
   to find one,
      but the odds are definitely better.

I have found several dozens of them
   in my many years of wanderings
      while watching myself looking for fish.

Mine are usually sandstone-worn, smooth,
   and have a subtle groove
      for the primal digit, the thumb.

Though tempted to skip it across water,
   one can pass many happy hours,
      pondering everything at once
         or nothing much whatsoever
         with that newfound friend
         to the sense of touch.

It'd make a great gift to a blood brother
    or to a country Miss or Mrs. or Ms.,
        if one can steal one's self to give it
            after exploring mysterious thickets.

Silver dollar-like, it easily slips into
    a pocket, fits flat against the thigh
        while one climbs an embankment…

Something There Is

in a whisper,
in hearing your name said softly,
lovingly, sincerely, divinely?
as from an angel hovering attentively
over your intuition.
Something there is therein
on one pivotal occasion
in the dark of dawn of day
that stirs you so deeply,
then gives you a vision
defying description or meaning or purpose,
and then the wonder
and then the questions
and then, eventually, the answers…
facing the day and the excitement
of experimental change
of becoming Silence,
of playing at being everything,
and then the being of Peace and Progress.
easily beyond all literature or speech.

It Is So Amazing

to have a body that one can evolve in,
feel thankful for, enjoy the senses,
knowing that it is growing healthier, younger,
toward blissful living, invincible Being.

It is so amazing to be alive toward forever
in service to ourselves and everything else,
animal, plant, mineral, spirit,
alive to life for deeds of genius (for heaven's sake),
for perfecting health, for perfecting works
during these scientific times
of perfecting understanding…

It is so amazing to have a caring family
and friends to be with for rest
and recreation,
to have loved ones one can Be with,
listen to, learn from,
while ever intrigued at emotions evoked
via varying moments of intersecting
circumstances,
seen in a lifesaving light,
buoyed by belief,
consoled by the soul's solace

eternity…

It is so good to see the stars of the day
and the light blue sky adorned by warblers, finches.
our playground of the amazing future,
the deep green trees, deep green leaves of lawns.
so good to inhale the colorful aromas of hyacinths,
syringas, gardenias, carnations, chrysanthemums…
to have it all to favor, look up to,
climb into, be shaded by, ascend to,
to love, and be loved by.
each leaf a flag of freedom,
each star a signpost for travel
in eternal Being…

Sanders, the Cat

is a live fly swatter. He stands up, reaching,
hooking into the curtain with one paw
while batting at them in the air
like Henry Aaron swatting homers.

Haven't had him very long.
A girl walked into the store where I worked
and asked if I knew of anyone who might like
a good cat. I took a peek in the cardboard box
and said, matter-of-factly, "I do."
She could hardly believe her ears, I thought.

He is black and white, but for the rest
of the shift, he was a bit gray at the assortment
of fingers poking around in the handle holes.
Occasionally he'd yowl in absolute terror.
I felt sorry for him. I felt his pain.
I told him so. Tried to console him.

Now, at home in the trailer, I call him mine,
but really, he's his.
Scarcely listens to a word I say.
The first day, he just prowled around meowing.
The second he spent looking out the window

with me at the wind and the rain.
By this time, we were fairly close friends,
so I took him outside awhile.
He just stood there on all fours, looking around,
not knowing which way to go.
I understood.

Several days later, on a Saturday, I believe,
I let him out again,
didn't see him until the next day.
He was lying on the front step,
smiling in the warm, inviting sunshine.
He smelled like perfume and slept all morning,
no doubt dreaming…

I's Rollin' Along

inside of a song, up over hills, and down dusty
dales, one mundane day (in my dreams) when I spies
the biggest, darn dust devil I ever laid my dry,
burnin' eyes on.
it was vacuumin' up farms and ranches and such,
wherever it went. I looked around for a basement,
a well, a ditch, or somethin'. I stopped my "bug"
and got out to dig a hole when it stole my handy
dandy army surplus shovel, which made a deep
impression on me. I considered seriously building
a bomb shelter just as soon as I arrived home to
my own private doorway, windowsill.
I's drivin' as fast as possible, but it wasn't
half fast enough as it was really breathin' down
my tucked in neck, the hottest, dustiest air you
ever coughed, inhaled in your life.
I's doin' fairly well, 'bout a hundred miles an
Hour, but as I glanced into the rearview mirror, I
could see I didn't have an hour to spare. I prayed
I wouldn't have a flat tire and hafta start wailin'
the "flat tire blues" again.
suddenly I got hit by a thought to stop and crawl
down under the "bug," but not before I tried to
use my teeshirt as a sail, the crazy little whirlwind

took my shirt, too, got a heckuva sandblastin'
for a bad idea…
Not good, I remember thinkin' as a shrill thrill
spiraled up my spine, my nervous system, so I slid
to a skiddin' halt and calmly slithered deftly
down beneath my four-speed transmission and
defiantly laughed. "Let that blizzardy wizard of
wind get me now!" But no sooner that I hollered
that, the bug just up and floated away,
like a magic carpet, a leaf, a bird…

I musta passed out 'cause when I came to,
I was feelin' a little depressed under six inches
or so of sand,
found my buggy on all fours, its top was torn off,
but I kinda liked it, always wanted a dune buggy,
a convertible!

We Had Been Revving

our engines for a long, long journey
in different directions.
We didn't exactly know what was keeping us
from peeling out of Mike's driveway.
Maybe we were waiting for the switch to click
in our intuitions.
Maybe Mercury had to quit retrograding.
Maybe there was a slippery snowstorm
on that Idaho horizon.
When business was finished per usual,
and all of our "goodbyes" were said or implied,
and we finally realized that no rope was tied
to either bumper,
long held feelings for new, familiar faces, places,
and tastes fueled us out of there, to new eras
in our respective lives, and from now on
until Enlightenment opens its sleepy eyes,
we will patiently practice liftoffs like the
legendary Pogo plane and/or rocket like a
satellite into a very short orbit
or slip like a ship down a chute to "new life"

No Birds Up Here

just high, azure sky
and a dreamy, wispy mattress of white vapor
to peer through…
cards anyone? Monopoly?
Past Philadelphia, I felt I could have played
chess or checkers on the distant landscape.

Having reread the magazine and rested my eyes,
I find I'm eager to get home to solitude.
The comedy station was a lot of laughs.

Observe the single seagull.
Its wings move ever so lightly as it glides
along, held aloft by tactile air.
Will this huge, "silver bird" follow suit?

It did.
It's a crisp morning here in "icicleville,"
"diesel city," Burlington, Iowa.
I'm over-rested, I guess,
awfully tired of waiting for planes and buses.

It's a crystal day out there.
No one seems to be in any kind of a hurry

Here, except me.
The bus is an unconcerned hour late
in "glitter city"

Finally on the freeway, home again to MIU,
Wind-sculpted snowdrifts gleam like diamonds,
a trifle too brilliant for my blue eyes.

O soul open to all…
All is open to you…

Halloween

It's a night owl's dream
for extra-excited tots, adolescents, and parents
  grouped up and taking turns knocking
    on likely-looking doors
      while a dog on a leash barks, barks, barks,
        all hollering pretty much in unison.
"TRICK OR TREAT!"
  for one sweetly scary evening
on a chilly November's eve
as a frigid wind moans, "Don't litter, please."

spooky ghouls, ghosts, skeletons, trolls, goblins,
  plastic pumpkins, fractured creatures
    walk and talk up and down the crableaf streets,
      admiring sculpted jack-o'-lanterns
        with various expressions on their
        glowing faces,
          most have lost some teeth
            on All Saints' Day's eve
              on Halloweennnn…

Wishful through the Window

blows the steel gray air,
blasts the sleet and the snow…

No sign of life out there,
except a few thousand mallards
wingin' it southward…

Pierce arrow winds try to drive away
with our lives,
even in libraries,
and with it goes the memorable warmth
reminding one of summer mornings
when we didn't need a woman's loving touch
quite so much.

Alone we are unto this life of cold,
or so it seems, sometimes
like an evergreen atop a mountaintop,
peering down upon the freeze sustained
by immortal beings going hither, and so
the cold winds blow against the panes…

"What?"
"Time to close?"

"I fell asleep?"

Streetlight moons be my guides tonight…

I feel so much better now out of doors…

The wind has gone down, gone to sleep.
Everyone's asleep…

        Light in this sea of night…
Serene to see the floating flakes of snow, I go
On and on and on into the acoustic night…

When Moose Soar in Spirit

Standing in icy water up past his knees,
He chews pine pitch,
Blows a nose bubble,
Eats very little,
Drinks sparingly,
Absentmindedly…

Scratches itches against solitary pines, fir,
Rolls in deep meadows of clover and buttercups
And poison ivy…

Gazes up at amber sunsets,
Combs antlers in wooded groves,
Ponders eternity beyond full moons…

<h1 style="text-align:center; font-style:italic">I'll Be Seein' You in My Dreams</h1>

"Ole Sol's" still shinin' through the pane.
Been puttin' off washin' the car,
Thinkin' it would rain.
Tomorrow, I've got to see about a job
To get me out of hot water at the bank.
Today, I found a place to stay,
But I only have God to thank.
I'll be seein' you in my dreams…

Last night, arm behind my back, I forced
Myself in to the dance, was carried away
By the vibrations in the region of the heart.
Stood there like a statue in a trance.
Girls were there to pick me up if I fell over.
The scene was a tragedy, I guess.
But I just couldn't quite let go.
I'll be seein' you in my dreams…

The stereo takes me back into the past.
Feelings come from somewhere, make me lonesome
For the comfort of your hand.
I wake up at night when I realize you're
Not here warm against my back.
Still, I know it will get better someday.

Ran into an old acquaintance of yours
At the laundramat. Damage was minimal.
She asked how you were.
I'll be seein' you in my dreams…

Had to turn the radio off.
It was two o'clock in the morning.
The lady upstairs was pacing the floor
Or something.
I'd been dreaming of you. You were smiling.
You were beautiful in your robe and bare feet.
Yes, I can believe it. It's just my luck of late.
Can't get back to sleep…
I'll be seeing you in my dreams…

My Friend, the Air Is Moving

luminous clouds are finally coming into view.
the trees are telling everyone the current news.
gusts of wind are ushering in a soothing thunderhead.
the rain is coming too…

"Ole Sol" has almost been unbearable
these last few weeks of August.
Mother Earth is dry and parched,
and the people seem very, very tired.
I wonder if the swallows
will make it back to Capistrano.

The neighborhood of leaves is weaving
to and fro. They blow and wave in unison,
"Hello." Bantering courageously, hopefully
regaining the spirit of living,
awaiting the blessed rain…

Four-o'clocks are nodding their heads,
drooping sunflowers, giraffe about the fence,
drying, browning leaves are parachuting out and

away from treetop lanes of view.
the summer season, it seems,
may be falling too…

Ahh…the rain…

The Tap of the Drops

of rain on the roof
bring an up of the cup
of contentment too.

From the top of the sleep
that I plopped in a whew
to the bottom of sodden flip-flop shoes
that dropped in a heap by the trudge
of feet too pooped
by the heart of a pump
pursued by dues…pay please,
the knot of a slip
of a hope for proof of honor,
order, and peace…
Seeing but searching
for a headrest…
or the reassurance of your lap, Love,
but I'm dearly "hip" to the tapioca "trip"
of your lips and tongue…
and but I know I think I'll never forget
the sense and senses
in letting go
and coming home again
to the tune of the taps

of the drops of the rain
on the roof of our home
of incense, friendship…
and we!

Spiral

Break out the suntea, and root beer…
It's overtime for a celebration.
Doesn't matter what down it is.
Doesn't even matter if we win or lose…
As long as Bonnie leads the cheers.

It'd been a really tough game.
A very persistent drizzle kept dripping down…
It was mud wrestling on the field…
A bad dream we nearly drowned in.
It was late in the fourth quarter…
We were down by a point…third and thirteen…
No one could easily breathe as I faded back to pass.
All receivers were going deep as I coolly scanned
The unified field, cranked up my arm, and let her go…
    (suspense)
So wonderful to watch…seconds passed…in that un-
Believable eternity…long arching spiral…
Just like on TV…
Finally it came down right through the split end's
Hands and off the defender's helmet to surprisingly
Land like a gift from heaven in the arms of Bonnie,
The new girl in school, cheering on the sidelines…
Of the field.

The rest is history as they say.
It's all down on film…recorded for hysterical
Posterity…
She sped out onto the field…just happened to be
Wearing my number. Zigzagged past opposing players,
Past incredulous officials, coaches, and screaming
Fans…right into the end zone…
Scoring the winning points.

After a little dance and giving the ball a spin,
She turned and faced the onrushing crowd with
Her arms in a V as both teams, laughing and
Talking, carried her off of the field.

Order was eventually restored.
We won the game on a last second kick.
The day was made complete when I asked her out
For ice cream. She said, "I guess."
Life is a sweet spiral…ever since…
(Alas, another dream)

Love
is the limb
the dove of peace
is perched upon…

that special something
giving support…
whenever we waver
in the wind.

Roll Up the Warmth, Please

please, these freezin' fingers
that can't seem to find the handle
to these fries and sandwich.

Brr…twenty degrees of frost…
watch me skip the root beer too,
a trifle too cool for this ice-cold kid
with clatterin' icicle incisors.

Mmm…ahh…hot, juicy soy burger
on dill pickle and lettuce
on mustardy ketchup
about to drip
into that lap. Whew…

So let us Chevrolet home
with all 350 cubes…
200 horses
of 35 mile an hour power
and jjjump iiin ttthe oven.

What Is the Wind?

Or who?
Who knows for certain?

It might be that the wind
Is the air of God's desire
To touch the world's children.

When gusts push against our ambitious progress,
Maybe it's his way of slowing us down, down, down
To sane, serene living.

When gusts give us a nudge,
Maybe it's His way of urging us onward,
Higher and higher mid-waves of limbs
Of poplars and elders.

It might be that that wind is merely the air
Of Mother Nature's dear desire
To clear the air for healthy living…
Or simply a celebration of a truly moving life.

Whatever the breeze may be…
We know it is.
We somehow sense its power.

It comes and goes regardless.
Blows hot and cold, warm and cool,
In careful yet carefree currents, caressing
Each and every color of hair and skin
Of every equal one.

Wandering where it wishes…
It must be free…

When We Were Kids

we'd head for the sleds
at the first sight of a white earth
knock off the cobwebs…
brush off the dust balls…
hurry up, and let's get goin'…
HiHo, here we go…headfirst sleddin'
down this foothill slope…

Trudgin' up another hill of fun…
pullin' that wooden crate was such a thrill,
dreamin' all the while how free we'd feel,
sailin' down that slippery hill…
HiHo, here we go…headfirst sleddin'
down this foothill slope…

Scooby dooby doo,…we'd buy an innertube
from the neighborhood service station,
and once we got a big, old tractor tube
and tied it on the back bumper…
two frozen tubers were plowin' through
snowdrifts, brush, and bushes…
every time the car towing us…
turned another corner…
Yes, HiHo, here we go…feet first flyin'

up this foothill road…

Once up on hilltop mountain,
we piled on, locked our arms, and gritted
our teeth, and some grinnin' wise guy
gave us a heckuva shove…
Boy, did we fly…
we were passin' every cup and saucer in sight…
surprised a kid on a carhood who flew faster
than he ever thought he would,
had a look of relief on his face
as we went by.
HiHo, here we go out of control
down this hilltop slope…

Round and round we turned…pickin' up speed…
unconcerned…enjoyin' the ride…
eyes opened wide, though, when we realized
there's a big canal down there.
everyone looked around for help.
HiHo, here we go headfirst to sure death,
down this foothill slope.

We were an unorthodox flyin' object
soarin' through the air.
but how can I describe the way we hit
the back of the canal, folded and kabonged
straight up into the wild, blue yonder.
when we finally came down, all I could hear
was moanin' as I's brushin' snow out of my eyes,
one or two were kinda laughin' as I checked to
see if I's in one piece. Yeah,
my watch was still tickin'.
HiHo, here we go headfirst diein'
down this foothill slope…

And so it'd go
all day long we did that,
slipslide up the long, glassy hill…

have a terrific ride,
crash into the canal,
then crawl around moanin' and laughin'
till no one was left who could crawl
or laugh or moannnn…
HiHo, there we went…headfirst flyin'…
down those foothill slopes…

—◦———❧◦◦◦❧———◦—

The Season of Autumn

is usually fruitful
when Mother Nature's seeds have seasoned…
and harvest time is plump and juicy
on the doorstep of the stormy future.

Sometimes the freeze comes early,
fruits then fall in slushy ooze…
evergreens, as always, are waiting ready
to smudge against the heaven's blues.
Wise old burdened oaks are aware, too,
that this is the time for giving…
all that meant so much…
all that makes life living.

Brown, crispy leaves…
sun-warmed memories…
deftly do they gently nestle
down upon the aging grasses,
there to die together,
there 'til death passes…
to seeds of greener pastures…
to worlds of graceful splendor…
beyond imagination…

Indian Summer

A very warm welcome…
a relaxing reprieve
from two-coat weather.

A seventy-degree day for raking leaves…
boys playfully kick a football
    and tackle the ballcarrier…
        cheerleaders sit at a card table,
            sip a cup o' tea leaves…
contemplative neighbors are in their yards,
    down on their knees, pulling weeds…
one fella rides around mulching leaves…
a few are in their gardens, harvesting
vegetables, leaves, and berries…

everyone seems to be enjoying one's self,
    in one way or another,
        as cares easily leave…
            on Indian Summer.

The Day Has Averaged

into evening…

Anywhere other than here…
Any instant other than this…
is far, too far for me.

You see?
I'm calm.
Unbelievably calm.
Calmer than I've ever been before.

Thoughts have vanished.

What one or two appear…
wander in just in time.

Narrow is the corridor…
unbounded is the hymn.

Who held those hands to here?
Just that typewriter.
Just this quiet.

The day was common:

delays middlemanning plans…
not enough time…
not enough patience…
not enough hands…
all stirring a potpourri of feelings…

Enjoyment is forever subtle, it seems,
and though the day has averaged into evening…
this night, this peace is somehow…
far above it all…

Individual Flakes of Snow

are taking their time descending down to terra firma,
imperceptibly whitening the rain-moist soil.
juncos titter and flit from limb to limb
of nameless bushes and brushes
about the house and grounds…
They are nimble little birds
of black and white and gray…
and they cheer up every winter morning,
adding a bit of lively magic
to these dark, December days…
To be so alert, so effortless, so harmless
seems a worthy wish for any day.

I think that I could sit for hours
enjoying their curious industry
in search of simple seeds
and their perfect tracks across the crust
of crispy snow
is a wonder to my heart,
and equal to any art of the earth or universe
or so, says my soul.

A Sense of Adventure

is the seventh sense.

It blooms in the springtime
after a cloistered winter of haphazardous,
yet easy-does-it, driving,
arriving early through the snow and bleak
of inhibition from the sixth intuition.

We have a feeling that there is more to life
than meets the eye.

Thanks to previous adventures
that know no seasons (in the unified field),
we have begun to sing of the inner sun
like the hummingbirds in the garden,
perched on the eave of eternal empathy
with reality's essence: simplicity…
sort of a honeysuckle summer
for life.

Enlightenment?

I long for You
as a loved one longs for a loved one.
I know I shouldn't,
but I do.
Impatiently patient,
I wait for You.
Steadfast, I cling to You,
my dream.

Can't help imagining
how it may be,
how You may be me,
I, Thee.

What a wonder it will be,
what a wonder
the first wonder of the world.

Will it be for me as it was with Whitman?
Bucke? Wordsworth? Shakespeare or Bacon?
and very many more?

Will I stand at the heart of life…
equal to my task yet so pleasantly detached?

completely pleased with the aims
of an almost effortless life…
and write
in a likewise timeless manner?

And last but not least…
will family and friends
soon follow?
lead?

From One

On a long journey to becoming all, the same as one, in a larger sense, fragile, Dewdrop plopped from the lowly leaf on which it lived and rested and has had its rebirth, becoming a part of a ribbon of agile water trinkling down from rarefied heights of quiet, joyous silence, in good time, merging in with sister springs all inspired to be content to be so slow in deepening down to widening realizations of living, colorful, greening growth, curious as it goes, gradually increasing speed. Dewdrop suddenly slips, dips over rapid river rock covered with carefree, slippery mossgreen mosses, falling down, down, down into a clearly deep and bubbling pool where it whirls deliriously round and round again and again until it dizzily settles for flowing, slowing to ponder roses wild and free on either side…

Little Dewdrop drifts directionless as black and gray vapors form undeniable power to pour their plaintive tears, pattering down upon all the seemingly infinite drops of sweet dew being nudged out into a torrent of frothing, roaring, flooding, fellow waters, unifying, giving way to the broadening, deepening, heightening river of changing times while calmly observing itself growing in self-awareness in the continual process amid all the barely perceptible on the way to greater depth of lapping waves of sea across a shifting, sandy beach, so pacified or full of peace, a kind of dying to the past, perhaps, though the moment has yet to arrive to rise as light and leaflike as a butterfly upon the curl of a breezy, happy, erratic flight to some other special here on an ever varying plane of ceaseless change or growth or evolution in heaven's name or God's all, as always, but just now, in innocent acceptance of one's simple self as a harmless drop of the basic stuff of everything on its very own way to being all or all-being, hence feeling liberated, surprising integrity of personality, joyful appreciation for life and the living, and somehow being more aware, more alive, more sincere in prayers of gratitude in timeless time…

I've Lived the Life

of the artist, an amateur scientist, intuitionist,
rarely dining in the finest "rest-all-you-wants."
far from starving though always thirsting…
spiritually speaking,
just doing my daily duty
for the duration of this truly
otherworldly opportunity
for continuous bliss…

hoping for wisdom by creative light
on blinding, bright mornings
or by moth orbits and lamp glow
on herbal tea evenings…

I aimed my pen toward farthest stars,
eased back the bow
as far as it would comfortably go
with the cards dealt me,
and a few more, thanks to Providence
and friends and family.
"I shot the moon," one could say
to coin a cliche'.

By some mysterious urge,

it was of what I could do
the most rewarding
in every sense of the word…
under every circumstance.

It was my best work made play
on and for our special
nondescript occasions.

Canine Conversations

Awaken the silence
As most of us dream in oblivion…

A few, perhaps, one at least, is listening…
Curiously…wonderingly…what are they uttering?

Acknowledging their accents and cadences
For phrases…I imagine they're telling tales
Four stories high. All told…
Or sharing the joy of a master joke or two
Or something silly they said or did the day
Before.

Even today I'd like to know what all that
Persistent barking is about.
Do they have thoughts and feelings too?

They're at it again.
The moon isn't even full.
They're out there in the cold and black,
Probably talking about the weather,
The economy, and whether we'll ever
Get out of the "red" without equal taxation.

Shorty

Shorty was a cool pooch.
   Long ears, long nose, long body,
      long hair, long tail, short legs.

We used to play tag around the apple tree…
   wrestle in the pasture…
      take long walks on sunny Sundays…
         pick asparagus on ditch banks…
            sneak up on ducks and geese…
               pick blackberries while swimming free…
                  listen to birdsongs…
                     build forts in distant woods

                        far…far from the peaceful farm

                           we roamed

Ponce de León

The courageous Spanish explorer would have gladly patted his paunch and pounced on the opportunity to transcend or reverse the aging process.

History books report that he looked high and low for the famed and fabled "Fountain of Youth," only to come up empty-handed. So what if he just happened to reexplore a healthy portion of southern North America. It wasn't what he went after.

Nevertheless, exploration must have been more than a little rewarding, walking around, poking flags in the ground, and making solemn declarations.

Exploration is a sacred practise, for sure, a natural product of "hope springs eternal"…

Maharishi Ayurveda

the timeless science of health
is reemerging from antiquity.

For the health of the people,
this ancient knowledge is being applied
as medicine in prevention of everything
other than optimum happiness.

Learn to balance the physiology
with common spices
from your spice rack.
Who says medicine has to taste bad
Or cost an arm and a leg?

One Bead of Bliss

More beautiful and valuable than a diamond,
Yet so like a diamond of morning dew,
Formed in their clear as crystal minds
And found its way directly down
Into a warm, mirrored pool
Within their hearts and souls.

Bliss arose…drifting higher…into their higher mind,
And higher to the light (like mist),
Touched them, kissed them, thrilled them
With radiant brilliance…
Filled them so very deeply, fully, richly…
With resonant silence…blessed peace…

Like children in new and profuse woods,
They innocently followed inspired streams
Of flowing, creative, celestial awareness…
Dreams turned in time to visions…
Visions turned in time to forms…

Joyful songs were sung into the fresh and open air…
Reverent psalms were whispered unto the heavens…
Similar to sunbeams through rainclouds in springtime.
Bliss refreshed their every dreamy breath…

For the rest of each of their loving days…
For the rest of each of their lovely nights…
And for the rest of all of our blessed lives…

When nineteen, I sat in the Boise State Library and prayed for guidance. I was up and headed toward the philosophy "stacks" and went around to the end where I saw a faded green cloth-bound book by Richard M. Bucke of Ontario, Canada. He had a two-hour revelatory experience that changed his life forever—and mine too.

About the Author

Bruce was born in Caldwell, Idaho, and raised in "Treasure Valley"—Boise, Emmett, and Middleton—where he studied farming, athletics, and scholarship. Phonics taught by Mrs. Turnbull flipped the switch decoding the mystery of English. He had great teachers, coaches, friends, and parents.

Thank you to Autumn and Stacy for your patient assistance at Newman springs.

Painting by Wendy Uhl